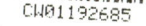

I SEE SCIENCE

STATES OF MATTER

DISCOVER THE SCIENCE ALL AROUND YOU

IZZI HOWELL

First published in Great Britain in 2022 by Wayland
Copyright © Hodder and Stoughton, 2022

Produced for Wayland by
White-Thomson Publishing Ltd
www.wtpub.co.uk

All rights reserved
HB ISBN 978 1 5263 1505 2
PB ISBN 978 1 5263 1506 9

Editor: Izzi Howell
Designer: Clare Nicholas
Series designer: Rocket Design (East Anglia) Ltd
All illustrations by Christos Skaltsas
All design elements from Shutterstock.

Printed in Dubai

MIX
Paper from responsible sources
FSC® C104740

Wayland
An imprint of
Hachette Children's Group
Part of Hodder and Stoughton
Carmelite House
50 Victoria Embankment
London EC4Y 0DZ

An Hachette UK Company
www.hachette.co.uk
www.hachettechildrens.co.uk

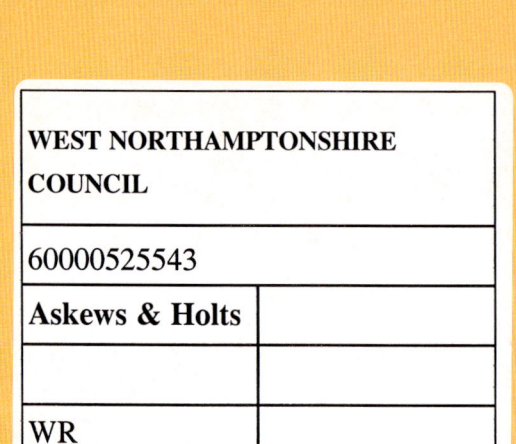

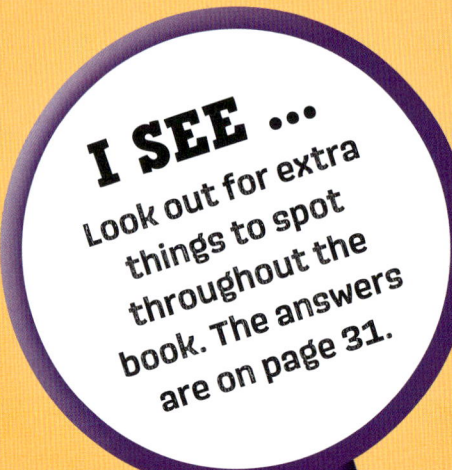

I SEE ...
Look out for extra things to spot throughout the book. The answers are on page 31.

WEST NORTHAMPTONSHIRE COUNCIL	
60000525543	
Askews & Holts	
WR	

CONTENTS

States of matter	4
Spotting solids	6
All about solids	8
Fill it up	10
All about liquids	12
Blow to inflate	14
All about gases	16
Hot and cold	18
All about melting and freezing	20
Wet and dry	22
All about boiling, evaporation and condensation	24
Rain to river	26
All about the water cycle	28
Glossary	30
Answers and further information	31
Index	32

STATES OF MATTER

Everything around us is made up of matter. There are three main states of matter:

Solids, such as a plastic mixing bowl

Liquids, such as orange juice

Gases, such as butane gas for cooking

Each state of matter has different properties. The wood that makes up this boat is a solid. It holds its shape.

Liquids, such as this spilled drink, flow and can be poured.

Gases float away and escape into the air.

Some materials change state at different temperatures. At around 30°C (the temperature on a very hot day), chocolate changes from a solid into a liquid.

5

SPOTTING SOLIDS

Many objects around the home are solids.

Plastic, metal and wood are all solid materials.

A solid object, such as this bowl, holds its shape.

Some solids, such as butter, can be cut.

A solid object, such as this cabinet, will always take up the same amount of space.

Grains of sugar are solids even though they can be poured.

7

ALL ABOUT SOLIDS

Solids stay the same – the same shape, the same size and in the same place!

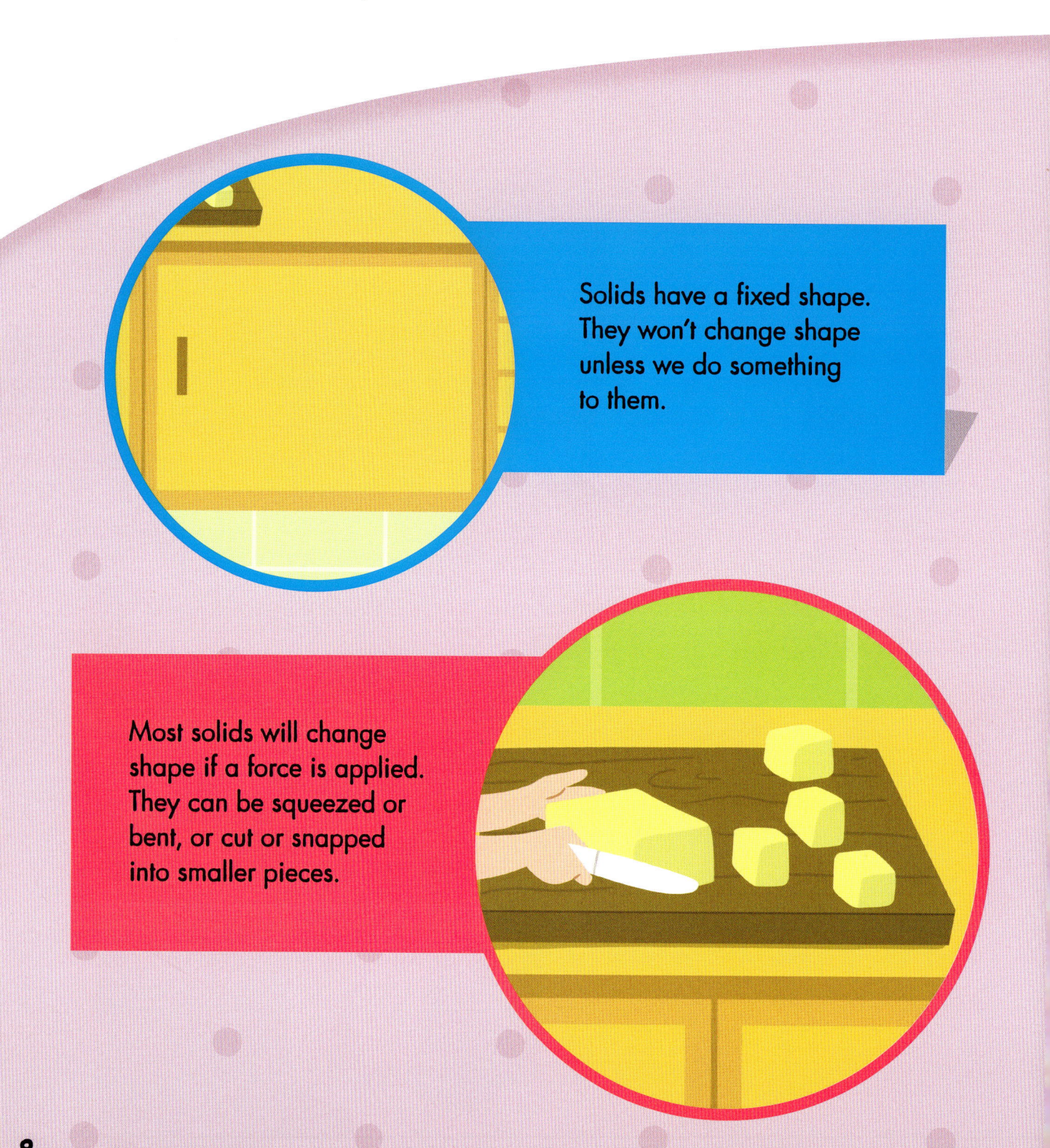

Solids have a fixed shape. They won't change shape unless we do something to them.

Most solids will change shape if a force is applied. They can be squeezed or bent, or cut or snapped into smaller pieces.

Solids always have the same volume. This means that they always take up the same amount of space.

Even though sugar, salt and sand can all be poured like a liquid, they are still solids. This is because they are made up of many tiny solid pieces that all hold their shape.

Most everyday materials are solids, such as wood, plastic, metal and fabric. Each material has its own properties, as well as the properties of a solid.

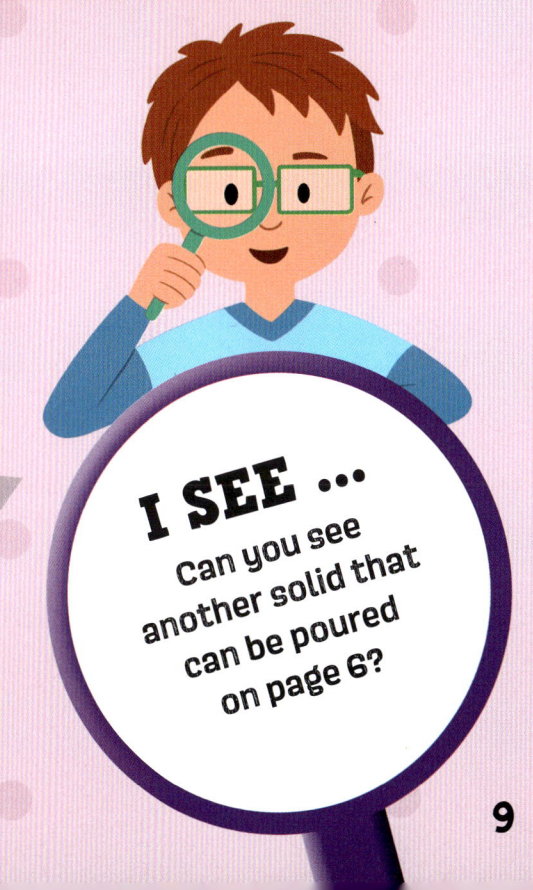

I SEE ...
Can you see another solid that can be poured on page 6?

9

FILL IT UP

Liquids flow and change shape.

A liquid can be poured.

A liquid takes the shape of any container it is placed in.

If a liquid isn't in a container, it will form a puddle.

10

Liquids always take up the same amount of space.

People need to drink liquids (mainly water) to stay healthy.

Water is a liquid at room temperature.

ALL ABOUT LIQUIDS

Liquids can change shape, but they always take up the same amount of space.

Liquids flow. This means that they can't be held, as they will fall through your fingers!

A liquid can take the shape of any container. If this smoothie were poured into a different glass, it would change shape to fill the new container.

If a liquid is not kept in a container, it will spread out to form a puddle or pool. Eventually the puddle will evaporate (see pages 22–25).

Liquids always have the same volume (take up the same amount of space). Liquids are usually measured in millilitres and litres, which are measurements of volume.

Water is a liquid at temperatures above 0°C and below 100°C. Other liquids at room temperature include milk, olive oil and juice.

I SEE …
Can you see another food that is liquid at warm temperatures on page 10?

BLOW TO INFLATE

Gases can escape and change shape. They can be hard to spot.

Gases will change their shape to fit inside different spaces.

A gas will escape out of an open container.

The air is made up of different types of gas.

Most gases are invisible.

Above 100°C, water turns into a gas called water vapour.

ALL ABOUT GASES

Gases behave differently to solids and liquids.

Gases can move around easily. They can change their shape to fit inside any container.

Unlike solids and liquids, gases expand to fill the space around them. If a gas is in a closed container, it will spread out to fill all the space available.

Gases can be squashed down to fit into smaller spaces, such as this gas canister. Special conditions are needed to shrink the gas to fit into the container.

Gases move around and float. They will escape out of any container that is not closed.

The air is made up of many different gases. It is mostly nitrogen, followed by oxygen. It also contains small amounts of carbon dioxide and water vapour.

I SEE ...

Can you see another drink that contains gas on page 14?

17

HOT AND COLD

Solids and liquids change state when they are heated and cooled.

Heat turns a solid into a liquid. This is called melting.

Ice melts into water at temperatures above 0°C.

Solids melt at different temperatures.

Cooling turns a liquid into a solid. This is called freezing.

Even metal, such as this fence, would melt if it got hot enough!

Water freezes at temperatures below 0°C.

ALL ABOUT MELTING AND FREEZING

Solids melt into liquids, and liquids freeze into solids.

When a solid heats up and reaches a certain temperature, it turns into a liquid. This temperature is known as the solid's melting point.

Different solids have different melting points. The melting point of water is 0°C. This is why water is always liquid at room temperature, unless the room is extremely cold!

Most metals have very high melting points. The melting point of iron is over 1,500°C, so iron only melts in special machines in factories.

Home freezers are cold enough to freeze many household liquids, such as water and milk. Other liquids, such as olive oil, may turn into solids at room temperature if it's cold enough.

A freezing point is the temperature at which a liquid turns into a solid. As with melting points, this is different for every material.

I SEE …
Can you see another frozen treat that will melt soon on page 18?

WET AND DRY

Heat can make liquids turn into gases.

Liquids slowly turn into gases when they are left out in the air.

Heat makes gases evaporate faster.

22

If you heat up a liquid to its boiling point, it will start to turn into a gas.

When gases cool down, they turn into liquids.

There are bubbles of gas in the boiling liquid.

Water vapour condenses into water when it touches the cool tiles.

ALL ABOUT BOILING, EVAPORATION AND CONDENSATION

Boiling and evaporation are two ways that liquids can turn into gases. Condensation is when a gas turns back into a liquid.

Each liquid has a different boiling point. Water boils at 100°C. Boiling water is very dangerous and will burn your skin. Always ask an adult to boil water for you and be careful around saucepans and kettles.

You can see bubbles of gas forming in a boiling liquid. The bubbles float to the surface because gases are lighter than liquids. The gas rises from the surface of the liquid and goes into the air.

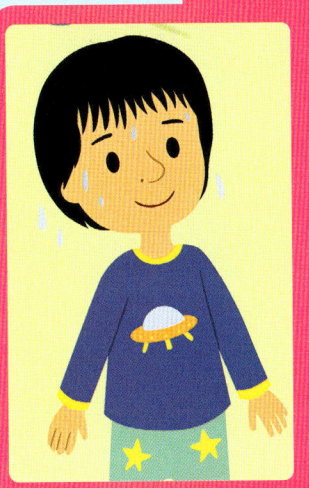

A liquid can also turn into a gas through a process called evaporation. This happens when a liquid is left out in the air, such as the water on this wet hair. Small amounts of liquid at the surface turn into gas and escape into the air.

Evaporation happens more quickly if the liquid is heated up. This is why a hair dryer makes hair dry faster, and why wet clothes dry faster outside on a hot, sunny day than on a cold, cloudy day.

When a gas cools down, some of it turns back into tiny drops of liquid. This is called condensation. We can't always see condensation happening because the tiny drops of liquid are carried away in the air.

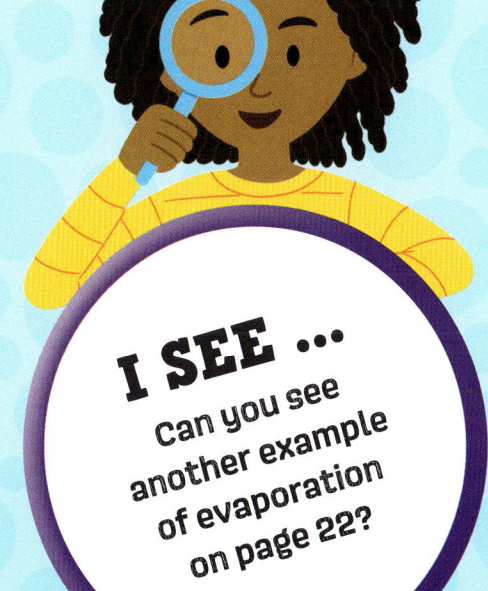

I SEE...

Can you see another example of evaporation on page 22?

RAIN TO RIVER

All of the water on Earth is constantly moving and changing state. This is known as the water cycle.

The Sun heats up water and makes it evaporate.

Water vapour condenses into clouds in the air.

There is water on Earth's surface in rivers, lakes and oceans.

26

Snow and ice on mountains melt and create rivers.

Rivers run into the ocean.

Rain and snow fall to the ground from clouds.

ALL ABOUT THE WATER CYCLE

Water exists in three different states in the water cycle.

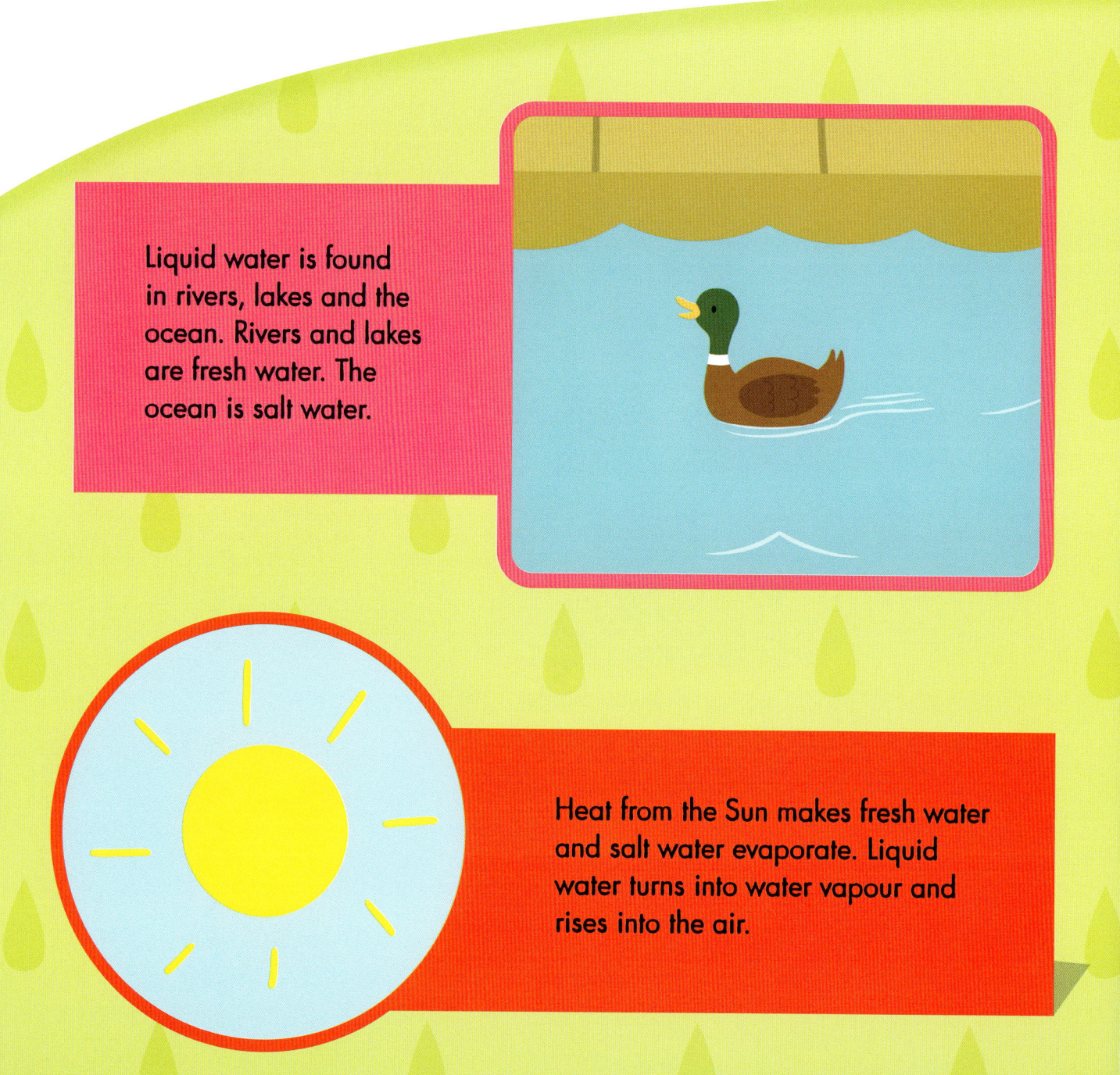

Liquid water is found in rivers, lakes and the ocean. Rivers and lakes are fresh water. The ocean is salt water.

Heat from the Sun makes fresh water and salt water evaporate. Liquid water turns into water vapour and rises into the air.

Water vapour cools down high in the sky. It condenses and turns back into drops of water. These drops of water come together to form clouds. When the drops of water become too heavy, they fall to the ground as rain.

In very cold places, rain freezes in the air and falls as hail and snow. These are both examples of solid water. Snow and ice are also found on the tops of high mountains.

The water from melting ice and snow on mountains flows into rivers, which are connected to the ocean. Water evaporates from these rivers and the ocean, and the water cycle starts again.

I SEE ...

Can you see another place where water will evaporate from on pages 26 and 27?

GLOSSARY

boil – to heat a liquid so that it starts to bubble and turn into a gas

boiling point – the temperature at which something boils

condense – to turn from a gas into a liquid

evaporate – to slowly change from a liquid into a gas

expand – to get bigger

freeze – to turn from a solid to a liquid

freezing point – the temperature at which something freezes

gas – something, such as air, that is neither a solid nor a liquid

liquid – something, such as milk, that is not a solid or a gas

melting point – the temperature at which something melts

melt – to turn from a solid to a liquid

property – a description of what a material or a state of matter is like

room temperature – the normal temperature inside a building that isn't very hot or very cold

shrink – to get smaller

solid – something, such as a piece of wood, that is not a liquid or a gas

state – whether something is a solid, a liquid or a gas

volume – how much space something takes up

water vapour – water in the form of gas

30

INDEX

air 5, 15, 17, 22, 24, 25, 26, 28, 29

boiling 23, 24
bubbles 23, 24

clouds 25, 26, 27, 29
condensation 23, 24, 25, 26, 29

evaporation 13, 22, 24, 25, 26, 28, 29

freezing 19, 20, 21, 29

gases 4, 5, 14–17, 22, 23, 24, 25, 26, 28, 29

ice 18, 27, 28, 29

liquids 4, 5, 9, 10–13, 16, 18, 19, 20, 21, 22, 23, 24, 25, 26, 28

melting 18, 19, 20, 21, 27, 29
metal 6, 9, 19, 21

pouring 5, 6, 9, 10, 12
properties 5, 9

snow 27, 29
solids 4, 5, 6–9, 16, 18, 19, 20, 21, 29
Sun 25, 26, 28

temperature 5, 11, 13, 18, 19, 20, 21

volume 9, 13

water 11, 13, 15, 17, 18, 19, 20, 21, 23, 24, 25, 26, 27, 28, 29
water cycle 26–29

ANSWERS

page 9: flour

page 13: honey

page 17: a fizzy drink

page 21: an ice lolly

page 25: a drying rack

page 29: a puddle on the floor

FURTHER INFORMATION

BOOKS

Investigating Solids (Be a Scientist) by Jacqui Bailey, Wayland, 2019

Solid, Liquid or Gas? (Get into Science) by Jane Lacey and Sernur Isik, Franklin Watts, 2020

States of Matter (Science in a Flash) by Georgia Amson-Bradshaw, Franklin Watts, 2018

WEBSITES

www.bbc.co.uk/bitesize/topics/zkgg87h/articles/z9ck9qt
Find out more about freezing and melting.

www.theschoolrun.com/what-are-states-of-matter
Discover more information about solids, liquids and gases.

www.dkfindout.com/uk/quiz/science/quiz-yourself-on-solids-liquids-and-gases/
Test your knowledge of states of matter with a quiz.

climatekids.nasa.gov/water-cycle/
Learn more about evaporation and condensation in the water cycle.